In God's Gentle Arms

In God's Gentle Arms

Richard Liddy

ARENA LETTRES
New Jersey

Copyright © 1979 by Arena Lettres

Printed in the United States of America

Library of Congress Catalog Card Number 79-88422

ISBN: 0-88479-022-3

For Mom and Dad,
my family
and all my friends,
among them, Jesus' mother

Das Ewig—Weibliche
zieht uns hinan.

"The eternal feminine
draws us heavenward."

Contents

Preface

In God's Gentle Arms is a kaleidoscope of images, insights and feelings that center around God's fierce and gentle love. At first I thought about calling it *Wrestling with God,* for much of it reflects a rather masculine struggle with the challenges of the divine. The present title, which was suggested to me by a friend, reflects a more feminine perspective: that the Lord intends to embrace us with his strong but gentle arms.

It consists of eight sections, each of which is focused on a key dimension of Christian faith. The Father, Jesus and the Spirit shed light on our own conversion of heart. This happens in the midst of community, in the midst of the Church. As we open up to the Lord in the intimacy of our personal relationships, prayer makes sense; the deepest love explains, supports and sustains all our other loving. Finally, this love keeps sending us out into the world to love in justice all our brothers and sisters. Obviously, the relations between these sections are not strictly logical and they can be read in any sequence.

This panorama of poems and essays mirrors, of course, my own life and my own experience. American Irish Catholicism, study for the priesthood in Rome during Vatican II, new movements in the Church, cultural transitions—all enter into it. Nevertheless, the deepest factors are the love and loves of my life. *In God's Gentle Arms* is written out of gratitude to a Lord who has loved me through the people he has placed in that life. Through them I have come to know him. *Ex abundantia cordis os loquitur.* From the abundance of the heart, the mouth speaks and the hand writes.

I have one suggestion about reading this book. Saint Augustine said: "Give me a lover and he'll know what I'm talking about." Hearts communicate through deeds, through silences and through words. I hope that my communion with the reader through these words will be rooted in the Lord.

What we have seen and heard
we are telling you
so that you too may be in union with us,
as we are in union
with the Father
and with his Son Jesus Christ.
We are writing this to you to make our joy complete.

[I John 1:3–4]

In God's Gentle Arms

I. FATHER

GOD

a phantom, an evanescent concept
not even a "breeze"?
For if a breeze, then moving and mover,
windmill energy,
water, power,
sailboat free,
fantastic, gentle
yet influential love.
A touch, not even an embrace,
a kiss on the cheek,
but meaning beyond words.
Soul-soaring, outward-breaking,
holy,
narrow, yet bubbling through and over.

Eternal.

Life.

THE STORY OF OUR SALVATION

The Scriptures are the story of a God deeply and passionately in love with his people. Love letters to his own, they testify to Israel's living experience of his intimate love:

> If Yahweh set his heart on you and chose you, it was not because you outnumbered other peoples: you were the least of all peoples. It was for love of you and to keep the oath he swore to your fathers that Yahweh brought you out with his mighty hand and redeemed you from the house of slavery.　　　　[Deut. 7:7–8]

The care, the intimacy and the guiding hand of Yahweh are constantly revealed in their history. And only the tenderest of images give a glimmer of the delicacy of his love in their lives. They suffered, they were in deep trouble, but the Lord granted them his protection.

> Say this to the House of Jacob, declare this to the sons of Israel, "You yourselves have seen what I did with the Egyptians, how I carried you on eagle's wings and brought you to myself."
> 　　　　[Exod. 19:4]

Human images, images of personal love, are favorites of Israel's writers and of her inspired prophets. The image of a mother, for example—the feminine tenderness of God—is celebrated by Isaiah:

> Does a woman forget her baby at the breast,
> or fail to cherish the son of her womb?
> Yet even if these forget,
> I will never forget you,
> See I have branded you on the palms of my
> hands.
> 　　　　[Isaiah 49:15–16]

4

The same tenderness is attributed to Yahweh as father:

> In the wilderness, too, you saw him: How Yahweh carried you, as a man carries his child, all along the road you travelled on the way to this place. [Deut. 1:31]

In no way did Yahweh want his people to die. In no way did he want them to drown in the waves of the sea around them. Rather, his whole concern was to show them the way to safety, security, the full and bountiful life—*shalom*! Today we would say "fulfillment," and whatever expresses the deepest dream of our heart.

Yahweh loved his people so much that he made them free and wanted to share with them the glory of true personal freedom. In so doing, he even allowed them to sin, risking their murmuring and rebellion. The Old Testament to a great extent is the story of Israel's failure to be aware of Yahweh's love.

Yet, even in their infidelity and idolatry, he was constantly present with them. He used the pedagogy of time and suffering. They experienced sin's dead end, but all the while he called out to them. He seduced his unfaithful bride, Israel, drawing her out into the desert where he could again in silence and nakedness speak to her heart.

> That is why I am going to lure her and lead her out into the wilderness and speak to her heart. . . . There she will respond to me as she did when she was young. . . . I will break bow, sword and battle in the country, and make her sleep secure. I will betroth you with integrity and justice, with tenderness and love: I will betroth you to myself with faithfulness, and you will come to know Yahweh. [Hosea 2:16–22]

God spoke in so many ways and at so many times to his people. He exhorted her, called out to her, invited her to share his freedom, to turn from her sins and know him as her true lover. Through admitting the error of her ways and turning to him, falling back in love with him, her sins, red as crimson, would become white as snow.

5

Come now, let us talk this over, says
Yahweh.
Though your sins are like scarlet,
they shall be white as snow;
though they are red as crimson,
they shall be like wool.

[Isaiah 1:18]

He spoke to the heart of the nation and said in so many ways, "How long, O Israel, how long?" He even promised a time in which he would give Israel a new heart, a heart of flesh to know him.

> I shall pour clean water over you and you will be cleansed; I shall cleanse you of all your defilement and all your idols. I shall give you a new heart, and put a new spirit in you; I shall remove the heart of stone from your bodies and give you a heart of flesh instead. I shall put my spirit in you; and make you keep my laws and sincerely respect my observances.   [Ezek. 36:25–27]

How could he implant this heart of flesh in the bodies of his people? How could he take out their hearts of stone? Only through the most radical step of all: "What more can I do for her that I have not done? I can send her my Son, my dearly beloved one. Through his experience of their lives from within, through his fidelity to me, through his loving and suffering and dying, I will show them how much, how very much I love them, how very passionate is my love."

On Good Friday, the Church speaks the words of the Father: "My people, what more could I do for you that I did not do?"

The Father could give us no greater gift than the gift of his Son. And the Son could give us no greater gift than the gift of his own life. To show us how much greater is the Father's love than we normally think, Jesus sealed the word of his life with the word of his death.

Father, let this chalice pass
Father, forgive them
Father, into your hands I commend my life
And I, if I be lifted up, will draw all people to myself.

The Spirit of Jesus is the Spirit of the Father's overflowing love for us. This love is eternally related to Jesus crucified and glorified. From his pierced side flow blood and water, John's symbol of the Holy Spirit (John 19:33–35).

There is no understanding this mystery. There is only "standing under" the cross of Jesus—which is our own cross. This love exposes the depths of darkness, the hatred of light in the world, the evil, even in our own hearts, that crucifies the good. But it also exposes the depth and height and breadth of love that embraces the evil ones and the instruments of their torture. Only through finding this love in the midst of this sorrow can we be called out of our own evil into the glorious freedom of the children of the Father.

Through the centuries, many mystics and saints have spoken of this mystery, this refreshing life that touches and flows through the crosses of our hearts. The Spirit of Jesus acts at the pinnacle of our soul and is experienced as peace, joy and the deepest fulfillment of our deepest human longing. Quietly, mostly imperceptibly, the Spirit of Jesus is the undertow beneath the ocean of the universe and of all our human cares and concerns. The books we read, our searching and our listening in prayer, our responding quietly, peacefully and courageously to all that is good are the province of the Spirit, the Spirit of Jesus which is the love that purifies, refines and inspires all our other loves. God's love comes to particular visibility in loving community life. Mutual care and forgiveness, even in the face of lovelessness, laying down our lives for one another, washing one another's feet—these are the actions and attitudes that incarnate the presence of Jesus' Spirit.

> If I, then, the Lord and Master, have washed your feet, you
> should wash each other's feet. [John 13:14]

This "music heard so deeply" is the Father's love in and through his beloved Son, Jesus Christ. The mystery of the universe, the mystery of our own lives, is that we are being invited to share in this eternal Trinitarian love. Through our living and loving and our love of the Father, through Jesus' presence in the Spirit with all our hearts and by joining the flow of that love in our own community lives, we can enter into the core of reality. We can experience, as Dante put it, the love that "moves the sun and the other stars."

Abba

Father, I am afraid of you . . .
     afraid of what might happen to me
     if I seek you:

     the pain . . .

     the humiliation . . .

     the dying . . .

     the future . . .

     even this day.

I am afraid I might be asked to suffer
     what Jesus suffered:
     humiliation and rejection . . .
     betrayal
     by friends . . .
     the loneliness of being misunderstood—
     being for you and
     accused of blasphemy . . .
Father, I find this fear in me
     of life
     of others
     of myself
     of you . . .
Father . . .   Father . . .

     Father me . . .

NOTHING CAN SEPARATE US

After saying this, what can we add? With God on our side
who can be against us?
Since God did not spare his own Son,
but gave him up
to benefit us all,
we may be certain, after such a gift,
that he will not refuse anything that he can give.
Could anyone accuse those that God has chosen?
When God acquits, could anyone condemn?
Could Christ Jesus? No!
He not only died for us—
he rose from the dead and there at God's right hand he
stands and pleads for us.
Nothing therefore can come between us and the love of Christ,
    even if we are troubled or worried,
    or being persecuted,
    or lacking food or clothes,
    or being threatened
    or even attacked.
As Scripture promised:
"For your sake we are being massacred daily and reckoned
as sheep for the slaughter."
These are the trials through which we triumph,
by the power of him who loved us.
For I am certain of this:
    neither death
    nor life,
    no angel,
    no prince,
    nothing that exists,
    nothing still to come,
    not any power or height or depth,
    nor any created thing,
can ever come between us
and the love of God made visible in Christ Jesus our Lord.

[Romans 8:31–39]

Perhaps the central question of our lives is this: What is the foundation of our faith? Or, to put it another way, what is the basic truth to be remembered in all kinds of trials? What belief can we build our lives on? What conviction can our hearts return to when everything seems confused?

The answer can be expressed very simply: We are specially loved by God our Father who in Jesus showed how much he loves us.

There are no limits to the Father's love save those we allow to come between us and an ever deeper belief in and experience of that love. Even there, his desire is to break down those limits gently, patiently and lovingly. The biggest barrier to this is a failure to believe that his love is infinite. It is a barrier that is shored up and solidified by the many things our emotions tell us as we face the pains and sufferings of life.

The title for a book on this subject might be *Lies My Emotions Tell Me*. Each day and many times a day we allow our emotions to face the difficulties of life by telling us, "You're a failure," "you're weak," "you're no good," "there's no way out." And we tend to leave it at that. The shocks to our nervous system, many of them natural dimensions of developing creation, are translated as, "You have so much to fear; doom is imminent." Often, the misunderstandings and slights of community living quickly turn into the visceral conviction, the feeling that no one loves me, no one cares for me personally. It's as if we had tape recordings in our minds and hearts that translate every small problem into a universal rejection.

A constant barrage of such emotional translations easily merges into the fundamental belief: "I am indeed unlovable—that's why no one loves me. I have nothing special or beautiful or God-given about me." The fear and fright at living with such a belief can easily result in unloving activity and behavior. If I have no personal dignity, why bother about living in a dignified way?

But what does the Word of God say about our reality? Perhaps it says something diametrically opposed to these messages. In his letter to the Romans, Paul speaks of our basic Christian

11

dignity. He tells us that God has poured his own love into our hearts through the Holy Spirit. He tells us that, therefore, we are his special children and can, with Jesus, speak to him as "Abba, Father," the intimate Aramaic expression for "Papa."

Because of this—because we are God's special children— Paul tells us that nothing can come between us and the love of God made visible in Christ Jesus our Lord. As you read Paul's eighth chapter you can sense the momentum of emotion as he reaches a crescendo, enumerating all the evils that cannot really come between us and the love of God.

A good examination for each one of us would be to go through this section of Paul and ask ourselves if we allow any of the things he enumerates to come between us and this deepest conviction, this basic belief, in God's passionate love for us.

With God on our side who can be against us?

Do we let the fear of people's opposition come between us and the belief in God's love?

Since God did not spare his own Son, but gave him up to benefit us all, we may be certain, after such a gift, that he will not refuse us anything he can give.

Do we fear that his grace will be lacking when we need it, that there is any limit to his gift-giving?

Could anyone accuse those that God has chosen? When God acquits, could anyone condemn? Could Christ Jesus? No! He not only died for us—he rose from the dead, and there at God's right hand he stands and pleads for us.

Do we think our own sins can separate us from God's love? Do we think they are too big even for his love to overcome and forgive? Could he care that much? Can our weaknesses, our failures and our personality defects separate us from a God who gave his only Son into our hands—a God who raised that Son to life where he now pleads so deeply for us?

12

Nothing, therefore, can come between us and the love of Christ

That's a big word—*nothing*. Perhaps we could let ourselves feel it in our very bones . . .

Even if we are troubled or worried

about ourselves or those whom we love

or being persecuted

in a thousand ways,

or lacking food or clothes

or have financial worries

or being threatened

by incomprehension or antagonisms

or even attacked,

This is always possible for those who live their lives for the truth, for Christ.

As Scripture promised: "For your sake we are being massacred daily, and reckoned as sheep for the slaughter."

Some, more sensitive than others, truly feel they are being daily massacred.

These are the trials through which we triumph by the power of him who loved us.

In this battle everything is working toward a triumph.

For I am certain of this:

I may not be certain of many things in life; there may be many areas of doubt, but of this I am certain:

Neither death

O Death, where is your sting?

Nor life

Sometimes harder than death—but again, where is your sting?

13

No angel
> No superhuman power, no evil conspiring spirit . . .

No prince
> No president, nor governor, nor mayor, no authority in this world . . .

Nothing that exists
> Nothing, nothing I've done or the world has done in the past . . .

Nothing still to come
> That meeting tomorrow, what so-and-so might do to me; what will I do when I grow old and retire? Will death be painful? Etc., etc. . . .

Not any power
> No obsession nor neurosis nor psychosis—no evil spirit at all, no bad habit . . .

Or height or depth
> No fate or guilt, no feeling of condemnation coming from within or from beyond me . . .

Nothing can ever come between us and the love of God made visible in Christ Jesus our Lord.

One feels like cheering as Paul reaches this pinnacle of praise for God's love. A standing ovation for the Father's love visible in Jesus would seem to be the fitting response. If that love is so good that it can surpass all these obstacles, then it is indeed great. The psalmists and liturgists through the ages have been truly correct in placing the sentiment and feeling of praise and thanksgiving at the core and center of Christian prayer.

The effect of God's infinite love breaking into our beliefs and hearts is to transform our feelings about who we are. Just as through the persistent, believing, accepting love of a young man, a young woman gradually can come to believe in herself as loved and lovable, so the Father's love aims at transforming our awareness of who we are. He aims to bring us to the realization of our great dignity as his children.

CHILDREN OF THE FATHER

A group of priests were sitting around one day discussing their problems. Finally, one spoke up emphatically:

> The important thing to remember is that we are *sons*—no matter what! We are sons of the Father. That's who we really are. No matter what we've done, no matter what problem we've had, no matter what sins we've committed, still, we are sons.

The others were stunned. Each left that meeting with a new lightness in his heart, a new conviction. Even nature looked brighter because each one at least faintly realized anew that this was a gift of the Father. There was a new lightness in their steps. There was a new love for other people. For the Father's special love for each of them made them more open to his special love for all.

II. JESUS

THE PERSON OF JESUS

Meaning, direction, love . . .
Three clues to a person,
Three dimensions of his identity.
His meaning,
the direction of his life,
the love of his heart.

"But who do you say that I am?"

Father, reveal Jesus to me
as you revealed him to Peter . . .
("No mere man has revealed this to you.")
Not just in mind
nor just in work
but also in heart.

PIERCED

At times·
the very side of the universe
is pierced open—
   a suffering
     an experience of intense love
     a word
and in the opening we catch a glimmer of
     the heart of God.

"Simeon blessed them and said to Mary his mother, 'You see this child: he is destined for the fall and for the rising of many in Israel, destined to be a sign that is rejected—and a sword will pierce your own soul too—so that the secret thoughts of many may be laid bare.' " (Luke 2:34–35)

"Now when all the people had been baptized and while Jesus after his own baptism was at prayer, heaven opened and the Holy Spirit descended on him in bodily shape, like a dove. And a voice came from heaven, 'You are my Son, the beloved; my favor rests on you.' " (Luke 3:21–22)

"At that, the veil of the Temple was torn in two from top to bottom; the earth quaked; the rocks were split; the tombs opened and the bodies of many holy men rose from the dead, and these, after his resurrection, came out of the tombs, entered the Holy City and appeared to a number of people." (Matt. 27:51–53)

"When they came to Jesus, they found he was already dead, and so instead of breaking his legs one of the soldiers pierced his side with a lance; and immediately there came out blood and water. This is the evidence of one who saw it—trustworthy evidence, and he knows he speaks the truth." (John 19:33–35)

FOLLOWING JESUS

All of us experience fear at the thought of following Jesus. We hesitate or pull back because our hearts are plagued with unvoiced anxieties about what a relationship with him involves. We are being invited to fall into the abyss of living warmth—and we hang back.

The first fear that faces us is fear of the cost. Following Jesus seems less meeting and walking with a person than it does performing all kinds of heroic and self-denying feats of moral living. We tend to think of the Christian life as "being good" or even "*really* being good," and such a project is exceedingly fearsome. We fear following Jesus and getting to know him personally because we mistake it for cold moral acrobatics.

Another, and perhaps deeper fear that keeps us from daily following Jesus is fear of ourselves. We know ourselves: we're sinners. If once we were to follow the high road of knowing and following him, we would certainly blow it. Only saints can follow that road, we tell ourselves; only those who are strong and good. I would be too embarrassed to follow Jesus. I'd embarrass him and his company of saints by my weakness. It is far safer to keep my distance, to be content with the low road of mediocrity, to leave Jesus "out there" where he is and be satisfied to stand by the door. I'd be mortified if I were caught as I really am!

Yet both these fears are pseudo-fears, illusions that the Prince of Darkness can sow to keep us from knowing the greatness of Jesus' love. For the real fact is—the *truth* is—that those who really follow Jesus, those who give him their hearts and know he is giving them his own heart, experience the demands of his love as joyful and beautiful. The weight of the world's laws is costly, but the love of Jesus is free and freeing.

Come to me all you who labour
and are overburdened,
and I will give you rest . . .
Yes, my yoke is easy and
my burden light.
[Matt. 11: 28-30]

The yoke of remaining apart from Jesus is difficult and the burden of living in this world on our own steam is heavy. The love of Jesus—being in love with him—does not remove the yoke or the burden of life, but it does make them easy and light.

Ask the saints. Paul traveled the Mediterranean world amid untold hardships. Love was his motivation: "The love of Christ compels me." Francis Xavier traveled from France to die in the Orient. He did so willingly and out of love. Saints who have literally given their lives for the sick or the poor certainly wouldn't depress you with the hardships of their working conditions. They would excite you and thrill you as they thrilled others with the lure of love that called them and fired them every day. The young Indian girls who give themselves to Mother Theresa's community for the poor of India are not frightened by the hardships but inspired by love. Many saints who performed heroic exploits for God and his people would probably tell us that it was so much easier than a job apart from Jesus—precisely because they were in love.

And what about the other fear, the fear of ourselves, of our own sinfulness? Here again, the saints would tell us that only in Jesus are we accepted as we are. Only he can take our bodily being, our sexuality and our emotions, and bring the good out of these divinely created dimensions of our being. Apart from Jesus' healing love, our emotions are confused, our sexuality turns inward toward ourselves and our bodily being dissipates. Jesus, incarnate Lover, wants to accept us as we are into his Body. Through his Body he wants us to know that we can afford to be known. With him, in the home of his love, we can be naked and unashamed. There we are "at home." We are for-

23

given, picked up, accepted and sent out to learn to love again. We can be free of our own embarrassment about ourselves before others because *the* Other has loved us specially.

Jesus, free us from these false fears that keep us from believing in the greatness of your love. Bring home to my mind and my heart the truth that the really costly life is the one apart from you. Show me that I need not fear your knowing me as I am—for you love me, *infinitely*.

THE FATHER SPEAKS

My child,
    My Son has already suffered the Cross.
    He has borne everything you have or
        possibly could suffer.
    I do not ask the same of you . . .
        He has already saved the world.
    All that I ask is that you let him use you
        to continue to save the world
        through his power.
    You know, or can know
        with a clarity he did not have
        in the Garden,
        on the Cross,
        that the story's ending is beautiful,
        that the story's ending is of a compassionate God,
        infinitely compassionate,
    Suffering your feelings with you
        close to you
        even when you feel far away.

GOOD SHEPHERD

Jesus forgives me my sins,
      is the mercy of the Father,
Good Shepherd, he picks me up
      in his strong and tender arms . . .
      he seeks me and finds me
      again and again and again.
      He speaks his word
      of dying and rising,
      of feeling the dying
      that is going on now
      and knowing he is here.

"Do not let your hearts be troubled.
Trust in God still,
and trust in me.

There are many rooms in my Father's house.
There's a room for you,
A place for you.

You are special in my Father's eyes
And in my eyes."

THE LOST SHEEP

"But you are the one whom I seek . . .

Every nook and cranny where you've roamed—
   sadness and pain unspoken, guilt unacknowledged—
   I have followed you, I am seeking you."

"But who will go with me on this journey into the deep?
   a man that is not afraid
   a man that somehow has been there
   'a man of sorrows and acquainted with infirmity'
   (the kid sitting all alone at the ball game)."

FRIEND AND BROTHER

Jesus, my friend, my brother—

my brother—related to me,
    a common life-blood,

my friend—caring deeply about every detail . . .
      my tiredness . . .
      when things happen quickly
      and quickly get beyond me . . .

III. SPIRIT

SYMBOLS

Water, washing
    flooding,

Fire, cast upon the earth . . .
    burning
    hearts,

A dove . . . gentle bird . . .
    descending

and
wind, blowing where it will . . .
    you hear its sound,
    but you cannot tell where it comes from
    or where it is going . . .
"That is how it is with all who are born of the Spirit."

Augustine's "More intimate to me than I am to myself."

The Spirit

    conspiring
    with our spirits
    to wake us up,
    to catch a glimpse
        of eternal vistas,

to know and speak
        the truth
        in love,

to repent,
to become
    more and more
    the New Creation . . .

Hints and guesses
    as to the Spirit's
    action and reaction,
"writing straight with crooked lines."
"The hint half guessed, the gift half understood, is Incarnation." (T.S. Eliot)

WRESTLING WITH GOD

That same night he rose, and taking his two wives and his two slave-girls and his eleven children he crossed the ford of the Jabbok. He took them and sent them across the stream and sent all his possessions over too. And Jacob was left alone.

And there was one that wrestled with him until daybreak who, seeing that he could not master him, struck him in the socket of his hip, and Jacob's hip was dislocated as he wrestled with him. He said, "Let me go, for day is breaking." But Jacob answered, "I will not let you go unless you bless me." He then asked, "What is your name?" "Jacob," he replied. He said, "Your name shall no longer be Jacob, but Israel, because you have been strong against God, you shall prevail against men."

[Genesis 32:23–30]

A famous philosopher-theologian, Alfred North Whitehead, once remarked that our experience of God often goes through three distinct stages: from "God the void" to "God the enemy" to "God the companion" in our suffering. Perhaps this division can give us some clue as to the ways in which this infinite and ever-present love dawns in our hearts.

In an age when people speak of "the death of God" and "the absence of God" it is not surprising to recognize those times in human experience when God appears to be very absent indeed. Life seems a meaningless void and its central symbol is nothingness. Religious beliefs might be present but they play no vital part in people's lives. God is present in the form of a yawning emptiness. The novels and other literature of our time give ample witness to this experience.

After experiencing the absence of God, many go through a period of wrestling with him, an experience of "God the enemy." Like Jacob wrestling with the angel, they turn their inner energies to struggling with the Lord:

Why did you do this to me?
Why did you take away this loved one?
Why did you make me this way? with unsatisfied needs?
Did you create me and give me this being only to
    frustrate me?
Why did you do this to me?

One of the most significant lines of the New Testament includes Jesus' words from the Cross: "My God, my God, why have you forsaken me?" Even *he* experienced these feelings of separation from and abandonment by the Father. They therefore are not unworthy of us.

In dealing with many people I have come to realize how very important it is to let people know that it is not only *o.k.*, but *essential* to wrestle with the living God. Many say, "Oh, I don't have a problem with God. It's people I have a problem with." But why is God letting you have a problem with people? What is he doing to you in this, to your heart? And if those people are members or leaders of his Church, it is even more important to struggle with him: "If this is *your* Church, what are you doing in it—why are you letting this happen?"

Finally, for those who allow themselves to go through this struggling with God—which is also a wrestling with their own hearts—God is often experienced as the "fellow companion" in their sufferings. The two disciples on the road to Emmaus were sharing with one another their broken hearts and their broken dreams. A third traveler joined them and asked what they were sharing. In that context they heard the words, "Was it not necessary that the Christ should suffer and so enter into his glory?" Then they recognized that it was Jesus with them in the breaking of the bread. How many people down through the centuries have had the same experience in the midst of sufferings shared with another—and the Other? "Were not our hearts burning within us as he shared with us on the way?" (Luke 24:32).

The experience of the Spirit of the Risen Jesus is the experience of this fellow companion in our suffering. It is the experience of the one who walks with us on our particular and unique journey to Emmaus, who questions us on our particular experience of the Crucifixion and "how it feels to us." It is the experience, too, of one who so shares with us our dying—which is a "being born"—that we really and truly know "it is Jesus and he lives!" As a friend of mine once said, "It's not the dying we're afraid of, it's accepting the new life." Sometimes we are so obsessed with our own dying that we miss the new life being opened up to us.

THE ANONYMOUS SPIRIT

The process we spoke of in the last section can take place in people's lives in quite an anonymous way. The Spirit can be at work even in the lives of those who do not know Jesus explicitly.

People do not always recognize that it is the living God with whom they are wrestling. But everyone seeks love and all seek meaning. That love and that meaning are to be found in the personal and inter-personal God: "You have made us for yourself, O Lord, and our hearts are restless until they rest in You." In many varied and mysterious ways the Spirit of the Father and the Son tugs inwardly in the hearts of all people. Bernard Lonergan describes this anonymous action of the Spirit:

> It is as though a room were filled with music though one can have no sure knowledge of its source. There is in the world, as it were, a charged field of love and meaning; here and there it reaches a notable intensity, but it is ever unobtrusive, hidden, inviting each of us to join. . . . And join we must if we are to perceive it, for our perceiving is through our own loving.[1]

The living God can work his transforming effect in quite an unrecognized way in the lives of those who experience his absence and wrestle with him. "Quietly, imperceptibly, there goes forward the transformation operated by the Kurios, but the delicacy, the gentleness, the deftness of his continual operation in us hides the operation from us.[2]

Only later, with Jacob who wrestled with the stranger, do they say, "God was in this spot and I knew it not!" It was the living God I experienced in this or that spot, in and through this or that suffering—and he cares for me! The Spirit of Jesus is

[1] *Method in Theology* (New York: The Seabury Press, 1972), p. 290.
[2] Bernard Lonergan, *Collection* (New York: Herder & Herder, 1966), p. 250.

intimately present to me, to my history! In ways we have all experienced, the love of God in Christ Jesus has been personally present to our minds and hearts. "But inasmuch as being in Christ Jesus is the being of subject," says Lonergan, the hand of the Lord ceases to be hidden.

> *In ways you have all experienced,* in ways some have experienced more frequently or more intensely than others, in ways you still have to experience and in ways none of us in this life will ever experience, the substance in Christ Jesus becomes the subject in Christ Jesus. For the love of God, being in love with God, can be as full and as dominant, as overwhelming and as lasting, an experience as human love.[3]

Today, there is talk among many Christians about the Baptism of the Holy Spirit, a release of the energy and power and wisdom of the Holy Spirit in a Christian's life. Usually this takes place in the context of a community of Christians who share, pray for and, quite often receive, a much deeper and more intimate awareness of the living God in their lives.

Could this be anything more, or anything less, than the fulfillment of the words of Saint Luke's Gospel?

> Ask, and it will be given to you;
> search, and you will find;
> knock, and the door will be opened to you . . .
> If you then, who are evil, know how to give your
> children what is good, how much more will the
> heavenly Father give the Holy Spirit to those
> who ask him!
>
> [Luke 11:9, 13]

[3] Ibid.

37

THE WORKS OF THE SPIRIT

The Scriptures tell us that the Father so loved the world that he gave us his only Son, Jesus. And this Son wanted so deeply to be the bearer of the Father's love to us in the midst of our suffering and our suffering feelings that he gave his life for us. On the one hand, the Cross is a symbol of the most terrible evil. On the other, Good Friday, the passion and the Cross of Jesus are the revelation of the Father's yearning and caring for his people. The Holy Spirit *is* this eternal passionate love expressed in Jesus. Both the Father and Jesus in their unity speak:

> We love you passionately . . .
>> yearning for you to be . . .
>> and to be good . . .
>> and to be fruitful—in all things . . .
> To have life
>> and to have it in abundance.
> This is the Spirit, *our* Spirit, we wish to give you.

This love of Father and Son is the most intense love in the universe. So intense, so ecstatic, in fact, that it overflows in creation:

> The heavens declare the glory of God,
> and the vault of heaven proclaims his handiwork.
> > [Psalm 19]

It overflows into the Incarnation and the New Creation. It overflows into a love that is ever after us, as Francis Thompson wrote in *The Hound of Heaven,*

> > With unhurrying chase
> > And unperturbed pace
> > Deliberate speed
> > Majestic instancy.

The meaning of that chase is to bring us to life, a heightened consciousness of the world around, a more decisive entry into its unfolding. The Holy Spirit wakes us up to the realities that perhaps always were around us but that we never had seen before. As T. S. Eliot reflected in *Little Gidding*:

> We shall not cease from exploration
> And the end of all our exploring
> Will be to arrive where we started
> And know the place for the first time.

The Spirit, as it unites Jesus and the Father in intense love, calls us also into unity. From our isolation and separation, from our alienation even from our deepest selves, we are being called into unity with Jesus and the Father. We are being called into unity with one another. Unity, in fact, is the sign to the world of Jesus' transcendent mission.

> May they be one.
> Father, may they be one in us,
> as you are in me and I am in you,
> so that the world may believe it was you who sent me.
>
> [John 17:21]

Since that is Jesus' prayer, it is eminently forceful and efficacious. In a real way it is beyond us. Yet we can take part in the answer to it by surrendering to the Spirit of Jesus and the Father in our community lives.

Saint Paul wrote to the Roman Christians: "God has poured out his love into our hearts by means of the Holy Spirit, who is God's gift to us." The image is one of overflowing, flooding water. For us to experience that flood within our hearts, the floodgates of our hearts need to be broken open.

Often this happens through suffering. Some people, in the midst of the sufferings of their lives have experienced, perhaps for the first time, a deep silence in which they *felt* the name "Father" or the name "Jesus." The center of Jesus' own heart carried this one word: "Father." The Spirit of the Father points our hearts to "Jesus."

39

The intense joy of the first Christians more than compensated for the intense pain they experienced in the death of Jesus. Their personal defenses had been broken down and the living God, whose plan it is to work through suffering, death and even sin, could flood into their lives and hearts.

The coming of the Spirit was an explosion that had repercussions in courageous witness to the Father's love of Jesus and in a spontaneous outbreak of brotherly love. The gift of the Spirit found expression in their falling-in-love with and being-in-love with one another. The fruits of the Holy Spirit—love, joy, peace, patience, self-control, etc. (Galatians 5)—were in their community because the Spirit of Jesus was in their hearts.

IV. CONVERSION

HOLY GOD

Lord, God, holy one

    holy eternal one,

Eternal passion

Eternally opposed to all half-measure
                        mediocrity

    Yet letting be,

Eternally opposed to Sin
       and all that is sinful, empty

Yearning . . .

    for our freedom:
"I have come that you might have life
    and have it in abundance . . . "
                [John 10:10]

THE MYSTERY OF EVIL

T. S. Eliot once noted that humankind cannot stand too much reality. There is among us a tremendous drive to downplay the existence of evil or sin. We prefer to "drift," tasting life's pleasures and joys, keeping our minds free from facing the darkness and confusion—until, that is, we come face to face with "the void" in our experience and in the world. Then, even though the weather may be sunny, our feelings can color everything with the dark cast of death. To appreciate the greatness of the Father's love we need to appreciate how he saves us in Christ. In fact, it is only because of the greatness of his love that we can dare to face the depths of evil in ourselves and in the world.

The mystery of evil penetrates life in a variety of forms and on various levels. We read about the most obvious in the daily newspapers: wars, thefts, murders, prostitution, etc. All these flow from underlying attitudes that are very common—even in our own hearts—from the same attitudes that destroy or corrupt our personal relationships. Hatred, envy, jealousy, lust and all the "capital sins" are attitudes of heart that can, and in time will, destroy community, divide families into warring individuals and countries into warring nations.

In her book *Eichmann in Jerusalem*, Hannah Arendt employed the phrase "the banality of evil." Great injustices, great evils such as Dauchau and Buchenwald, can be propagated through people who, like ourselves, are "just doing our job," never looking at the bigger picture, but simply drifting along in an "ordinary" way. Is it not possible that the great symbols of evil—wars, concentration camps, the murder of the innocent—are really representative of what goes on in families, in small towns, in the personal relationships of each of us? Are not the scriptural images of hell, "the weeping and gnashing of teeth," an expression of what some people experience in their hearts even now? "Hell is other people," remarks Sartre in one of his plays, and he testifies to the slimy sense of evil which is like a jelly surrounding human existence and from which there is "no exit." As the prophet Isaiah noted: "Darkness covers the earth and thick clouds cover the peoples."

A century ago, long before the "death of God" writers made the "absence of God" a popular theme, John Henry Newman described the condition of the society of his day. He wrote of the "heart-piercing, reason-bewildering fact" that for many it is impossible to find God in the world.

> Either there is no Creator, or this living society of man is in a true sense discarded from his presence. . . . If there be a God, *since* there is a God, the human race is implicated in some terrible aboriginal calamity.[4]

Such is the human condition. Such is the "slant" of human society.

To speak to this human condition, Saint Paul in the first chapter of his letter to the Romans describes what he considers the basic and most fundamental attitude responsible for individual sins and the continuing cycle of sin and evil in the world. After enumerating various individual sins, he notes that these come from what he calls "futile thinking," "senseless minds," "base minds." A contemporary writer speaks of the condition in this way: "For among the evils that afflict man, none is graver than the erroneous beliefs which at once distort his mind and make systematic the aberrations of his conduct."[5]

For Paul, any attitude that does not "reverence God," acknowledge him and thank him for his gifts is an erroneous belief. Although people can know God—for he is present in creation—many do not honor him or give him thanks. Instead, they make the works of their own hands idols that replace the living God. "Claiming to be wise, they became fools." Their sin is say-

---

[4] *Apologia Pro Vita Sua* (New York: Doubleday, 1956), p. 320.
[5] Bernard Lonergan, *Insight* (New York: Philosophical Library, 1957), p. 687.

ing a basic "No!" to God. Because of this he lets them go their own way. Three times Paul follows up this attitude with the consequence: "Therefore God gave them up to the lusts of their hearts . . . to dishonorable passions . . . to a base mind and improper conduct."

In Romans 1 (20–21, 24–25) he observes:

> Ever since God created the world his everlasting power and deity —however invisible—have been there for the mind to see in the things he has made. That is why such people are without excuse: they knew God and yet they refused to honor him as God or to thank him; instead they made nonsense out of logic and their empty minds were darkened. . . . That is why God left them to their filthy enjoyments and the practices with which they dishonor their own bodies, since they have given up divine truth for a lie and have worshipped and served creatures instead of the creator, who is blessed forever.

Immorality then—and Paul includes all types in his list —is a result not just of weak will power but, more fundamentally, of a lack of a living relationship to the living-saving God. Deep reverence, faith in the Good News of his love and mercy, is the way to a whole and holy life.

Perhaps the reason the human condition is not more alarming to more people is that, not vitally believing in God, they do not believe in themselves. With no sense of their own God-given dignity, there is little awareness of their less-than-dignified condition.

> For if one is not haunted by the sublime about man, one does not know the humiliation either. One does not feel the Fall.[6]

Complacency and apathy mean that the human person has stopped dreaming. Visions and dreams of what could be have dried up and people conclude that "that's the way it is." "It's only natural —only human—for each of us to be out for ourself alone."

[6] Aelred Squire, *Asking the Fathers* (New York: Morehouse-Barlow, 1973), p. 27.

Saint Iranaeus conceived of Adam's fall as a rigid adolescent unwillingness to grow in a trusting relationship to the living God. Adam's sin was a hard-hearted and stiff-necked insistence on not growing in this ever new relationship with God. A rigid insistence on his own way cut him off from a deeper growth in knowing God and genuinely "growing up."

On the other hand, according to Iranaeus, redemption in Jesus Christ is a dismantling of such adolescent rigidity and fear in a free relationship with God. Redemption in Jesus is "becoming as a little child," free, trusting, lovingly relating to the Father. It is beginning anew, this time allowing God to be God and ourselves to be led in growth by him.

The mission of Jesus was to reveal us to ourselves, to bring out into the light the perversion of values in our souls, to call us to the Father's saving love. Jesus taught in so many ways that our "normal" attitudes and values are all upside down. We are grasping and competitive and angry. He taught us to be poor, to take the last place, not to worry, to trust in the Father's love. He came to convert our "slant" away from God and from one another back toward a slant in his direction and the direction of one another.

Redemption is God's love flooding our hearts. It brings us to a belief in love; it allows our hopes and dreams to be fed by the infinite Spirit. It involves a conversion of our whole being to knowing and being who we are in the universe, in Christ, in God.

"Intimations"

Planning to beat him out before he gets me first . . .

Worries
    about being beaten by so and so . . .
        or so and so . . .
    about money . . .

I've worked hard . . . I deserve a break . . . all systems go!

Don't bother about what he says . . .
    Don't bother about what she says . . .

Who cares?

SIN AND HOLINESS

What is sin?

Slavery and fear

sensuality, obsessions

not contributing
not attending to
the unending needs of those around . . .

unfree
bound, binding patterns . . .

("Bad habits come in on horseback and
depart flat-footed")

poor timing . . .

Not facing my own humanity

admitting
acknowledging
before others

as I ask them to help me
sort out the pieces . . .

perhaps becoming content

So that I may become free.

Holiness?
Dependence on the living almighty God
for our hearts to become free.

CONVERSION

To speak of conversion is to speak of our own hearts. It is to speak of their tendency to be hard and icy. It is to speak of their becoming hearts of flesh, warm hearts, hearts of love.

This human process, to which the Scriptures constantly point, means a radical shift in focus, a "waking up," whereby we come to know the Father's intimate love in the very core of our being. The great saints were converts. Having tasted the bittersweet quality of things without God, they found themselves grasped from behind by the Lord of life. As Saint Augustine said: "I went further and further away from you, but you came closer and closer to me."

Radical and ongoing. To speak of conversion as a turning around to the living God is, in a real way, to speak of an all-or-nothing event. Death has no degrees. Nor do "leaving all," radical poverty and loving with all one's being. The Gospel cannot be read without seeing on every page this all-or-nothing character, this radical call to return "today" to the arms of the Prodigal Father.

At the same time, the Father gives his children freedom—freedom to wander far from him, freedom to try things away from his presence, freedom to center in and concentrate on one's own attainments and enjoyments. Not surprisingly, as often happens, our consciousness contracts, our pleasures and enjoyments decrease and finally disappear altogether. It is this lost, sorrowful, self-contained person that today is called back to the Father. Sorrow and suffering are merciful indicators that we cannot save ourselves. We need to surrender to another who alone can save us.

John Henry Newman expresses the essence of conversion as this surrender of one's whole being, one's whole self, to the living God.

When a man comes to God to be saved, then I say the essence of true conversion is surrender of himself, an unreserved unconditional surrender, and this is a saying which most men who come to God cannot receive: they wish to be saved, but in their own way. They wish, as it were to capitulate, but upon terms, to carry off their goods with them.[7]

This surrender to the Lord can happen dramatically, as in the case of the Prodigal Son or in the lives of the great converts. It also can happen very undramatically, in the course of each new season of our lives. For each cycle of our lives presents us with a new self to give the Father. We have grown intellectually and in our talents. Our influence has prospered or waned and we have suffered or rejoiced. We are asked to give it all to the Lord, to surrender ourselves to him *today*. Perhaps I have been blessed with great opportunities, many friends and various talents. If I hug these to myself and live self-reliantly alone, I will die. This day I am asked to give up all so that I might receive all anew from the Lord of life.

If I do this and counter each failure with renewed commitment, then I will live. Then someone examining my life from afar may discern the hand of the divine Potter molding the rough clay of my life into a finer shape, firing the form into more pronounced lines—even perhaps breaking an imperfect effort in order to start anew on a clearer reflection of his living idea. From within, my life can seem a series of failures, the same problems faced again and again. But living life as a gift from and for the Lord, I cannot help being changed, being converted on ever deeper levels.

Everything can remain the same, even my actions; but everything is really different because *I* am different: my attitudes, my heart, my way of looking at things. A difficult life borne with heartsick bitterness can become a life borne with God-given peace.

[7] *Parochial and Plain Sermons* (London: Longmans, Green, 1896), vol. 5, pp. 241–42.

This process can go on in a hidden and anonymous way. But it can also at times become mysteriously clear that it is the Spirit of the living Lord at work in my being and in my history. Paul, Augustine, Ignatius and countless other saints recalled those "conversion moments" when the Lord showed them that it was his love at work in them. The stories of others are less spectacular. Still, it would seem the Lord's clear desire to make his hand more and more evident in the "turnings" of our human lives.

Mystery. All this can be pure poetry, literary dressing on humdrum reality. It also can be the scriptural record of God's desire to turn us to himself and reveal the deepest and fullest reality in our lives, the deepest dimension of our hearts and of the universe.

To say that this is mystery is not to indicate merely our lack of understanding but also the reality that is in itself so luminous, so filled with the light of God that we are dazzled and blinded by its brilliance. The eyes of our hearts are like those of an owl in daylight. Used to the darkness, we barely catch a glimmer of the divine process at work. That glimmer might be the awareness that patience is entering in where previously there had been impatience or that pride is giving way to humble self-acceptance. It may be that joy and deep peace are taking the place of agitation, that clarity of vision is replacing confusion or that commitment to the Body of Christ is supplanting disdainful criticism. The attraction of love may motivate us ever more widely and deeply. Most of all, the living Jesus is loved more fully in himself and in his people. All these, and others, are signs of the freely accepted change of heart wrought by the Spirit of Jesus.

Resistance and preaching. One of the major aspects of conversion is our resistance to it. "The Light came into the world but men preferred the darkness." Resistance to prayer and religious practices and the avoidance of people who might challenge us through their example and words can constitute a radical resistance to *the* Word. When preached, the Word can sting. It can cut through our preconceived securities, block our escapes, knock our feet out from under us. We can fall and in our falling trust very little that such humiliation might be the beginning of falling in love.

Again, this is mystery. Why is it that so often we can "hear and not understand," that a dimension of our spirit hates to hear the truth of our being? Only the mystery of sin and evil can explain this rift in our very selves.

This is why the Word of God is so important. Jesus preached parables and stories to bring his listeners gently around to accepting their own blindness and their need for salvation. The man of today similarly needs to be confronted with the wounds of his nature and the living Lord as his Savior.

Such preaching happens not just on Sundays and in formal classes. It takes on life much more effectively when embodied in the lives of concrete persons. The Word preached Sundays in the pulpit must first take root in the lives and relationships of the rectory and the pastoral team. That is the Word incarnate.

In the Church. The process of conversion, then, demands a willingness to repent, a willingness to accept the self one really is—wounded, poor, in need of God. Conversion demands facing the issues: the hurts, the pains, the failures, the sin. Genuine prayer, retreats and religious practices are not escapes. They involve the healing pain of facing and accepting our wounds in the light of God's love.

T. S. Eliot wrote that "the way down is the way up." In this acceptance of our depths, the presence of another human is central. "Confess your sins to one another, and pray for one another, so that you will be healed" (James 5:16). This is the place of the Church in the process of conversion. It is here that we can meet concretely and historically and be touched by and accepted by Christ, the Sacrament of God's concrete love. The Church is meant to be the expression of God's taking us up

53

into a new way of living, a Jesus-living that contrasts with the values and systems lived by previously. Joseph Ratzinger writes that,

> Whoever accepted the creed renounced at the same time the laws of the world to which he belonged; he renounced the worship of the ruling political power on which the late Roman empire rested, he renounced the worship of pleasure, and the cult of fear and superstition that ruled the world. It was no coincidence that the struggle over Christianity . . . grew into a struggle over the whole shape of life in the ancient world.[8]

Small communities, friendships in the Lord, renewed and renewing parishes—all these are the divinely intended means of our conversion. Learning to live with, accept and love one another is the most efficacious way the Lord has of re-forming our hearts in his own image. The sacrament of community living is the principal way in which the Lord purifies us and turns our hearts to him.

In the Catholic tradition the Sacrament of Reconciliation has been a major means of opening our hearts to the Lord in the midst of his people. Any priest who has heard the confession of someone who sees himself as a great sinner cannot help but be filled with the compassion and mercy of Christ. As is often quoted, "There is more joy in heaven over one sinner. . . . " That joy flows into the heart of the sinner as the love of the Father invites us to him. Even in this, our part is surrender, a letting go of ourselves as we know them. With that, we can find ourselves anew in the arms of another. To face one's life, to open one's heart to another, is to confess that one's center is not in oneself but in *the* Other. It is to give up everything in order to be open to receiving everything as new, a gift and a grace.

The Church is the community of the converted. It is the community of those who have turned around to the love of the

---

[8] *Introduction to Christianity* (New York: Herder and Herder, 1970), p. 74.

Father in Jesus. Just to turn to him in our hearts is to begin our journey toward him. It is to open ourselves to his attractive and attracting love.

> What no eye has seen, nor ear heard,
> nor the heart of man conceived,
> what God has prepared for those who love him,
> God has revealed to us through the Spirit.
>
> [1 Cor. 2:9–10]

SURRENDER INTO ANOTHER'S ARMS

It is because of a massive and pervasive resistance to the light of truth and love that moments of conversion are often spoken of as moments of surrender. After lengthy and devious resistance, after fleeing "down the labyrinthian ways of my own mind," the human spirit gives up trying and opens itself to the healing power of the Father.

William James analyzed such a conversion. After continually fighting with its weakness and impotence, the "sick soul" is brought to the point where it gives up. It finds it simply impossible to save itself and therefore casts itself upon the mercy of the universe, of the living God. It is precisely at such moments, it seems, that many great conversions take place. Precisely then, often in the midst of despair, a new and higher emotion enters in, a new peace and joy releases the Spirit from its bondage. This often occurs through the mediation of another's hand. James likens this process to the attempt to remember a name one "should know." The harder we concentrate, the more difficult it is to recall! Often what is needed is a relaxing of the spirit, a good sleep, for example, then in the morning—"out of nowhere"—and without any effort, the name comes into the consciousness. Similarly, religious conversions often require a "letting go," a surrender of the self-centered need to save oneself and the relaxation into the arms of another. James quotes the often-told story of the man who at night found himself slipping down the side of a precipice:

> At last he caught a branch which stopped his fall, and remained clinging to it in misery for hours. But finally his fingers had to loose their hold, and with a despairing farewell to life, he let himself drop. He fell just six inches. If he had given up the struggle earlier, his agony would have been spared. As the mother earth received him, so the preachers tell us, will the everlasting arms receive *us* if we confide absolutely in them, and give up the he-

56

reditary habit of relying on our personal strength, with its precautions that cannot shelter and safeguards that never save.[9]

One is reminded of Paul's conversion: "Saul, Saul, why are you persecuting me? It is hard for you, kicking like this against the goad" (Acts 26:14). Apparently the Lord had been goading Paul for quite a while and his fanatical resistance had resulted only in hurting himself. That goading was perhaps a series of incidents, the successes of the Christians—their example—his own inner fear of losing control, so many drops of water that only increased his fanatical resistance until he could resist no longer. He surrendered and that surrender took him into the arms of the Christian community, into the desert of Arabia to consolidate his conversion and, finally, to the ends of the civilized world to preach the Good News of Jesus Christ.

[9] *The Varieties of Human Experience* (New York: Mentor Books, 1958), p. 98.

LIBERATION
(John 20:19–20)

Free me, Lord, as you freed your apostles,
   from all those emotions that make me cringe inwardly,
   cowardly, fearful . . .
   afraid of myself
   and afraid of others.

Free me from that cowering feeling of wanting to remain
         hidden,
   afraid of being seen openly and publicly,
   afraid of being known by other people.
   "The doors were closed in the room where the disciples
   were for fear of the Jews."

Free me from the fear of making a fool of myself,
   of taking the first step,
   of initiating the conversation,
   of changing my mind and heart.

Let me breathe, dear Lord, the pure, clear air of your
freedom,
   the freedom you won
   by being true
   to your Father's love, and to who you really were—
   through death.

Let your freedom flow through me—
   to be faithful and loving to you,
   and to the person or persons I meet
   in each situation.

Free me, Lord, from the inhibiting influence of my friends,
     from the subservient account of the "significant others"
          in my life,
     from living totally dependent on what they'll think
     and what they'll feel
     about what I say and do.

Free me to be truly faithful to them
     by sometimes breaking their expectations of me
     and by being true to your presence in me.

Free me to rejoice playfully in your creation
     and in your re-creation,
     in the simple things like flowers,
     and beautiful sounds, and music that joys the heart;
     in people who see differently and in different ways than
          I do,
     and thus see more than I do.

Let me listen,
     and let me use your eyes to see
     more than my own little world.

Pry me open to your Spirit
     flooding my heart,
     with the great world, the new creation
     you are sharing each day with me.
     Allow me to be pried open by you.

Free me, Lord, to fall in love with—
     and be in love with—you.

Free me from worries about my problems,
     from a morbid preoccupation with self,
     from my past and my future,
     from a deadly seriousness about everything.

59

Free me to laugh and to cry,
to plunge through the cross and crosses of life,
and to know and hear your risen words
from the wounded and victorious person you are:
"Peace be to you."

Free me from hanging on to images, standards, and attitudes
of purely human success,
so that,
being free to lose all,
my heart may be open to receiving all
this day;
and to knowing that this day
all things—
all that comes my way in nature and persons—
all things are mine,
and I am yours
and you are the Father's.

                              Alleluia!   Alleluia!

HEALING

Healing is possible,

    it is available

Through the Spirit

    present in our midst

      as we are present
      to each other
      in love.

Just by being together

    in mutual acceptance,

The Spirit enlivens the creativity

    and gifts
    (that differ)

    in each one of us.

And our gifts

    are at the service
    of each other.

OUR YES

The Lord's care—

making his presence to us

    dependent on us.
The angel waiting on Mary . . .

"Peter, do you love me?" . . .

So dependent on our "yes," our real "yes,"

    needing us

    vulnerable . . .

V. CHURCH

THE CHURCH

The age of the Church
    its stability
    its tradition:
    a testimony that relationships can last?
    over time?
    over ages?
The Light, the Sun (Son)
    shining on the Church
    illuminating her
    lighting up her dark corners
    bringing forth her ancient meaning.
Gently dying at your hand,
    today,
    incomprehensible
    yet present.
Called "absurd" when you're not known . . .
    called "love" when you are.

SACRAMENT

Reality,

The Transcendent,

    acting
Really,

Independently
    of our acts
        and
    our plans

Yet entering
    our acts
        and
    our plans.

"This is my body . . .
    Do this in memory of me."

    "Whose sins you shall forgive, they are forgiven . . . "

"And I am with you . . . "

"Put your finger here; Look, here are my hands.

    Give me your hand; put it into my side . . . "

PERSONAL LOVE THROUGH THE CHURCH

One of the most beautiful of modern love stories is that of *The Man of La Mancha*. Particularly beautiful is the love of the wild romantic, Don Quixote, for the hardened woman of the streets, Aldonza. When he calls her a princess, she calls him crazy. When he sees her as beautiful, she reacts with violence.

Only gradually, through Don Quixote's persistent love, does Aldonza dare to believe in herself. Only gradually does she take the leap in faith, leave behind her identity as Aldonza, and assume that of Dulcinea, the sweet one. Through his love, she begins to accept herself as he sees her, as warm and lovable, beautiful and dignified. This is asking a lot of her, but love can accomplish it. It can bring out more life and beauty than we ever dreamed possible.

Is it too much to suggest that the love of the Father for us is a similar transforming love? Jesus saw in Peter and the Apostles more possibilities than the authorities of this world did. Regardless of their bumbling and shortsightedness, their fears and anxieties, even their weaknesses and betrayal, he saw in them the specially beloved of the Father. He saw the ones specially chosen to carry on his vision of transforming love. The result of his belief was their transformation into joyous, fearless proclaimers of the Good News.

Just as Jesus was *the* sacrament, the outward sign and embodiment of God's great love for his people, so the Apostles and the Church were to be the Sacrament, the outward sign of Christ. Just as he reached out and touched men and healed them, so the mission of Christ's body is to reach out and touch the human family with God's healing love.

By his acceptance of the elderly sick woman, by his pointing to the Father's special love for her, the priest or minister in the hospital room mediates God's peace to a person in need. He asks her to trust his vision of her as experiencing the very sufferings of Christ. In her he himself meets Christ. His trust in the Risen Lord carries her even through death. It can be similar in other situations: a father with his children, a woman with neighbors in need.

The Father's transforming love through the Body of Christ is primarily a life of love. The sinner who pours out his guilt before another lays himself open to Christ himself, who loved to be with sinners. It is in and through the Church—her Word, her sacraments, and her Life—that we experience the love of Christ. Through it we pass on Christ's special love to one another and to the world.

This flow of God's special love through the Church is not magical or superstitious. It is not a matter of rites and rituals that would make of God and people mere computers and automata. It is primarily a matter of the heart, a question of personal love communicated through personal contact. The contact can be minimal, as minimal as a touch or a word, but when that touch or word is infused with love, then Christ is specially present—touching, healing.

The sacraments and sacramental rites of the Church are the tip of the iceberg whose submerged base is made up of the give-and-take of divinely human love. Such rites express, deepen and strengthen the already present flow of forgiveness and love that constitute our interpersonal lives and reveal the mystery of personal love through Christ and through the Church.

Our major sin may not be what we often think it is. It may be hiding from the Lord's love in Christ and in his Church. A woman once told the story of how she disobeyed her parents as a little child by playing on top of a haystack. When she fell off and hurt herself, she was so frightened they would find out that she hid all day in a closet where no one could find her. Similarly, like Adam in the Garden, we hide from the only one or ones who can heal us. We hide from those persons who most can accept us as sinners, love us and recall us to wholeness. We hide from the Church, which can heal us. In doing so we hide from friendship in Christ, a friendship that means sharing the suffering of Christ so that we may also share his glory. As John Henry Newman wrote:

> Perhaps the reason why the standard of holiness among us is so low, why our attainments are so poor, our own view of truth so dim, our belief so unreal, our general notions so artificial and external, is this: *We have each the same secret* and we keep it to ourselves and we fear that as a cause of estrangement which would really be a bond of union. We do not probe the wounds of our nature thoroughly as did Augustine. . . . We may clean the outside of things. We are amiable and friendly to each other in words and deeds but our love is not enlarged, our affections are straightened, and we fear to let the intercourse begin at the root. And in consequence our religion as non-interior is hollow.[10]

If we ourselves do not experience a life of deep personal friendship and sharing, how can we deeply feel and sense the Lord's personal love for us? If we do not learn how to receive love from the Church, how can we in turn become "Don Quixote lovers" to the many "Aldonzas" in this world? If the Lord does not break through the pride that keeps us from one another, that keeps us even from *telling* one another of our need for love and support, then how can the Lord's love flow through the veins of his Body in this world?

The Lord has so loved us that he has placed his own life in our midst. We are so greatly privileged! We have the dignity of being channels of his redeeming love to one another. A smile, a word of encouragement, a service rendered—each small or large gesture in our lives can be the Lord's way of gently touching those we meet. Through us he accepts them, weak and human as they are, into his all-encompassing love.

Asked about the will of God—"Just what is God's will for us?"—a great preacher replied: "Did you ever think that God's will for you might be what you yourself want from the bottom

[10] *Christian Sympathy: Parochial and Plain Sermons V* (London: Longmans, Green, 1896), pp. 26–27.

of your heart?" Could it be that the God who created us set into our own hearts at their deepest level a vision of that "hundred-fold in this life," that community of love and friendship that is indeed a taste of heaven?

What do we really want out of life? Isn't it some form of community in the Lord? Could the Father be so loving that he might want to give us at least a taste of just that?

ALL THESE PEOPLE, LORD

All these people, Lord,
    Whom you love tenderly
        warmly
    As warmly as a woman in a man's arms . . .
Could you love us that much?
    Say to us
    Out of *desire*
"I love you . . . "
Wanting, willing, warming . . .
"I love you
    . . . want you
To be . . . you
    whom I've—we've made
    in our own image . . .

Male and female, we made you
    and love you
Into being . . . who you are,
Vibrant, pulsating,
    hungering, longing
For one another . . . ?"

Communion
    life hearts
    In You!

BODILY RELIGION

In Graham Greene's beautiful novel *The End of the Affair*, the heroine, caught between husband and lover, says this about her visit to a Catholic Church:

> When I came in and sat down and looked around I realized it was a Roman church, full of plaster statues and bad art, realistic art. I hated the statues, the crucifix, all the emphasis on the human body. I was trying to escape from the human body and all it needed. I thought I could believe in some kind of God that bore no relation to ourselves, something vague, amorphous, cosmic . . . like a powerful vapour. . . . One day . . . I would escape myself forever. And then I came into that dark church in Park Road and saw the bodies standing around me on all the altars—the hideous plaster statues with their complacent faces—and I remembered that they believed in the resurrection of the body, the body I wanted destroyed forever. I had done so much injury with this body. How could I preserve any of it for eternity?[11]

Many people seem embarrassed about the body, or have a mental tendency to skip over it. With that, perhaps, they forget themselves, for the body is central to Christian belief: "the resurrection of the body," "incarnation," "this is my body given for you," "the body of Christ." All are central to the Christian message. Perhaps what the world needs more than ever today is a "bodily" religion, a religion that affects a person so deeply that it can even affect the way he looks, so deeply that he can possess his body in peace and one day (or many days) "put his body on the line."

Certainly, a Christian would not hesitate to assert with Paul that "God is spirit." But it is also a fact that we are incarnate spirits, "body-subjects." The union of our spirits with the

[11] *The End of the Affair* (New York: The Viking Press, 1951), p. 133.

Holy Spirit is activated and finds expression in the signs, postures, places, times and symbolic gestures of our bodies. All these can—and it seems the Lord wills them to—incarnate whole depths of meaning in a person's life. Graham Greene's heroine continues to ponder on the body as the way we love, if only "sleeve against sleeve." Then she leaves the church. "In defiance of Henry and all the reasonable and detached, I did what I had seen people do in Spanish churches: I dipped my finger in the so-called holy water and made a kind of cross on my forehead."

Holy water, the sign of the Cross. They are gentle indications to oneself and to the world of the meaning of one's life, one's vision of "who I am" and "where I stand" in the total scheme of things. In Greene's case, the woman was "trying on" symbols expressing a meaning for her own life; she was washed by the waters of the Holy Spirit, sharing in the Cross of Christ.

It is because we are bodily beings that we need these symbols so much; they are symbols that touch our hearts. Every level of our being comes together in them: spiritual and intellectual, psychic and physical. "It is through symbols that mind and body, mind and heart, heart and body communicate," says Bernard Lonergan.[12]

The Scriptures portray Jesus healing people through touch, laying his hands upon them, putting his finger in a deaf man's ear, touching a mute man's tongue. Once he made a paste of mud and spittle and placed it on a blind man's eyes. There were many ways he healed through his bodily presence. And, today, many scientists tell of the healing power of touch. According to John V. Taylor,

> More and more practitioners are coming to recognize that the little-known dynamics of our interpersonal relations are the clue to a great deal of healing. We are discovering the therapy of touch, which is a sacrament of acceptance and love.[13]

[12] *Method in Theology* (New York: Seabury Press, 1972), p. 67.
[13] *The Go-Between God* (Philadelphia: Fortress Press, 1972), p. 212.

Little wonder, then, that Christianity is a sacramental religion. It involves the belief that God wants to touch us just as Jesus touched the people he cured. Washing, anointing, laying on of hands, feeding people: these are bodily ways of loving people, influencing them, touching them.

The symbol of the body in Christianity, then, implies an approach to the human person with *all* the dimensions of his being, all his concrete relationships and all his concrete means of communication. It includes the gestures and "body-language" that originate and ground the "vibrations" picked up by other people, whether of love or of acceptance and vulnerability or of defensiveness and closedness. It includes the meaning of one's life as incarnated in one's lifestyle. At the Last Supper Jesus summed up his whole life when he said, "This is my Body given for you."

Today, both some popular religious movements and "old-fashioned" devotions are criticized for one or another theological reason. Yet, for their adherents, they often *work*! Things happen in people's lives: cures from drug addiction, alcoholism or various sexual deviations; and, most of all, the formation of committed communities. A power is found in these "bodies" that, as one priest mentioned recently,

> you just don't find in many local Churches. People with these problems we send to psychiatrists and hope for the best—a verdict that is often a seal of despair for many.

In his *Varieties of Religious Experience*, William James noted that the cure for human problems must come in as strong a form as the complaint. In the case of acute psychological depression only the freedom of the expressive "bodily" type of religion can touch the deepest levels of the psyche:

> How irrelevantly remote seem all our refined optimisms and intellectual and moral consolations in the presence of a need of help like this. Here is the real core of the religious problem: Help! help! No prophet can claim to bring a final message unless he says things that will have the sound of reality in the ears of victims such as these. But the deliverance must come in as strong a form

74

as the complaint, if it is to take effect: and that seems a reason why the coarser religions, revivalistic, orgiastic, with blood and miracles and supernatural operations, may possibly never be displaced. Some constitutions need them too much.[14]

The Christian vision, then, is of God intensely involved in the human condition. The tender involvement of this God allows us and wants us to be free, to be lovers, to be channels and instruments of his healing love for one another. As Jesus was the sacrament of the Father's love to us, so we as members of his Body, the Church, are called to be the sacrament of his healing love to one another and to the world. That call is a summons to radical love.

Because creation is so vast and many-splendored, there are many levels on which the free flow of love can be blocked. Among them are poor self-images, the result of many implicit "put-downs": "You're no good; you have nothing to offer." "There's nothing beautiful in you to love." Such suggestions can escalate into self-defeating solutions of anger and violence. Wounded hearts and minds generate vicious circles of "solutions" that only deepen the guilt, the worry and the pessimism. What is needed so much is the "healing of memories" that releases the God-given freedom of the human spirit.

Human society and culture can solidify and intensify the individual's wounds by failing to understand, by being as "selfish" communally as the individual is personally, by manipulating people and not respecting them as basically free and called to freedom. The tyranny of many "shoulds" can be imposed upon people without pointing to any power to fulfill those "shoulds." Most of all, by its misjudgments and pessimistic views of reality, human society and culture can confirm people's basic negative feelings about themselves. Such pessimistic world-views or pseudo-solutions concerning the human condition constitute the realm of darkness that Jesus came to pierce with the Good News of God's healing love: "But if it is through

[14] *Varieties of Religious Experience* (New York: Mentor Books, 1958), p. 137.

75

the finger of God that I cast out devils: then know that the kingdom of God has overtaken you" (Luke 11:20).

On each of these levels, then—personal, social and cultural —people need to be touched. Some literally need a hand on their shoulder, a "holy kiss," a hug (1 Thess. 5:26; 1 Peter 5:14; Romans 16:16; 1 Cor. 16:20; 2 Cor. 13:12). Others, perhaps, need more to be "touched," to be "moved," by our word, by our acceptance of their minds and hearts, by the vision we communicate of what reality is about. To be appreciated as a thinking, free person is perhaps our highest compliment to them. To speak the word of the Father making others truly wise and free in Jesus is our greatest gift.

Indeed, the development and conversion of our lives is a growing refinement in our ways of "bodily" loving. Initially, our ways of loving can be very physical indeed. Later, a single flower, a kiss or a word can incarnate a whole heart of love. As we grow, such love can find increasingly simple and ordinary ways to reveal itself and to heal.

Jesus' desire to heal physically in the Gospel is not a magic show or spectacular "sign and wonder." His physical healing is part of a much deeper and wider healing. Bodily healing was in continuity with the psychic healing of the human person and, most of all, with the healing of the basic human vision of God's desire to love us and free us to love in community. Jesus touched people physically so that he could touch them in a deeper way. He told the woman at the well about her five husbands in order to tell her that he wanted to touch her in an even more intimate way. He healed through the communion of love.

What is becoming evident now is that the world today needs the same healing presence through the community of healers called the Body of Christ. This includes not just priests and ministers but a whole "body" of people where the sick and the lonely and the alienated can be "at home" both with God and with at least some others who understand and accept them. Here, in the context of warm personal relationships, people can share the belief that God really loves us and wants to heal us

76

through love. He wants to love us into loving. Here, faith is affirmed in the power of Jesus to heal not just physical problems but more especially wounded personal relationships and basic life vision.

But the Church is not just a conglomeration of saints but a large net that includes all kinds of fish. Many of them are in need of great healing themselves. They are so overcome with their own wounds, so self-centered, that they do not know themselves as healers of others. They are not free. Even our formation and education within the Church can seem a series of "shoulds," absolute moral demands with no awareness of the need for power to fulfill them. Moralism is a far cry from Gospel. The Good News is that God loves us as we are, as his beloved sons and daughters, and that he wants to love us into a far deeper loving than any law can encompass. The Church expresses the healing love of the one "who loves to hang around with sinners and eats with them" as well as the absolute demands of the Ten Commandments. That is why the healing works of the Church must go on in bars and in clubs and at meal tables, not only in the public liturgy of the Church. The public liturgy is only the beginning, the public expression of the healing, bodily-touching love that goes on in myriad personal and often hidden ways. Sometimes they are found in the healing power of personal relationships, sometimes in the healing of memories. Only the security that is the Lord can free us to communicate honestly about our need to be more and more deeply healed.

Communion and communication in the Body of Christ is the way of casting out unclean spirits and simply being loved into living out one's God-given vocation. This is why small groups can be particularly effective in the healing ministry of the Church. In such intentional communities, entered into freely as adults, we take on the sins and burdens of one another. Just as Jesus suffered freely and willingly within his own body the evil forces of ignorance and pent-up anger, so all of us ultimately are called to carry the Cross of our own situation, a situation humanly and Christianly constituted by bonds of love. With Jesus we are called upon, not to return evil with evil, but to overcome evil with good. We are called to love so much that we take people within ourselves, where they can experience transforming love. This is victimal loving. We need the eternal Father's passion empowering us into this type of loving: "No one takes my life from me; I lay it down freely of my own accord. . . . This is my Body given for you."

CONFLICT: PATH OF CONVERSION

Most of us avoid conflict like the plague. We flee suffering of any kind and during our formative years build all sorts of barriers and protectors to prevent us from suffering. Physical sufferings are bad enough, but personal and community-related ones are the major fears of our lives. If my viewpoint is not accepted, my weakness not taken into account, my person threatened by undignified treatment, then my whole being quakes.

The reason for these conflicts is the innumerable ways in which our hearts are formed. There are so many levels of feeling and aspiration, so many possibilities of experience. She's a woman and I'm a man: Who can adequately say all that goes into that difference? He has had little education and I've had a great deal. He's suffered personal hurt and tragedy and my life has been virtually unharmed. He's a liberal and I'm a conservative. All of these aspects—and many others—reflect dimensions of our lives and our hearts. On any one of them my heart may conflict with similar levels in another's heart.

The conflicts that spark the deepest controversy and bitterness, however, are those that center around the dimensions of truth, goodness and love. We may be one in what we eat or the style of clothes we wear. We may both be Italians or Irish or French, but the differences that divide us most radically are those of vision as to what is genuinely true and real, what is good and worth loving. Our rival definitions of reality and love, our idea of the meaning and truth of human life—these are the dimensions of difference and conflict that most tend to divide human community, that most accentuate the division among persons.

One thing that is particularly important is our vision of the totality of life. Is there a God or isn't there? Does he love us? How? Where? What does it mean to love God? Does it include loving people? What is love? How can individuals find God's guidance? Do any people or communities speak his word?

Political issues also may reflect our vision of what is basically true and loving. Are the leaders of my community guided by truth or not, by political expediency or by human compassion? Differences on such issues and modes of behavior can tear apart human hearts and human communities. It is no wonder that it's so often considered bad manners to discuss religion or politics!

For Christians, Christ Jesus is the basic norm for dealing with such conflict in community. It is the Spirit of Jesus that can bring life out of it, most of all by gradually convincing us that we need constantly to be saved, to be healed in our basic vision of the truth and reality of human community. We tend to see such conflict in community in one-dimensional terms. The enemy is "out there," in those who disagree with me, those who, by their rival definitions of reality and value, conflict with my priorities. It's all very simple. If only so-and-so saw things my way, if only those others would come around to my way of seeing things, everything would be all right. Everything —everyone—would fall into its right place, my place.

Such a one-dimensional vision is the source of much of the bitterness and anger in human community. If my vision and truth are unconditionally the vision and truth, then dissenters must be persecuted. My position must be defended and I must do that most defensively. Opposed to this is a multidimensional view which sees the Spirit working in an infinite variety of ways and conflict in community as a challenge to growth and conversion both for myself and for others. I cannot compromise the truth I see; to do that would be infidelity to that truth. But I am called to growth in vision, to ways of seeing what others see and what initially is hidden from my eyes.

There are different types of human personality and various people are variously gifted by the Spirit of the living God. Women often see dimensions of reality that many men do not see. Artists and poets see dimensions of life that frequently escape others. Such diversity can give us a clue as to the wonderful variety among persons and their insights into the many complexities of reality.

What is needed, then, is a sharing of vision that enables me to see what you see and you to see new things through my vision. What is not needed is the assumption that my vision is the total vision or that I have nothing more to learn.

It is important to *listen*. When we pray, God is kind enough to listen to us. So, in our relationships, one of the kindest and most loving things we can do for our brothers and sisters is just to listen to them, really listen, so that, with time, we perhaps can hear what their hearts are actually saying. This might mean spending time with them. It might mean spending time in prayerful solitude in which the Spirit can reveal to us what is being said to us by the hearts of the community around us. Such solitude generates patience, the ability to "suffer" the wounds of others.

A multi-dimensional view of conflict in human community can open us up to ways of differing in human community that go beyond head-on confrontation. My judgment can be absolutely correct, but quite often it is not the only relevant judgment in the situation. Others also can have judgments that are correct, and only patience and time will allow us to "see" the truth of their viewpoints. Sometimes various steps are needed before we can begin to see with another's eyes or they with ours. Premature confrontation can send us back to building barricades for our position. Reality is so much greater than what our limited vision is capable of; only cooperative sharing of sight and insight can open it to us. The French writer Simone Weil often wrote of "waiting on truth" as it dawns upon us.

This vision of conflict as a means of growth in human community presupposes an underlying attraction of our spirits to truth, reality and genuine love. The ability to endure tension but not break this underlying communion with others requires levels of human communion from which to begin. Most of all it presupposes the attraction of the Spirit of Truth and Love by which we are drawn out of our self-centered viewpoints and our refusal to learn from others into sharing a common "wonderful" vision of reality. The Spirit even can guide us as to when and where we can undefensively share our view of the living God and his living community.

Communion and actual community will come through conflict when we allow our hearts to forgive others sometimes just "for being who they are"; that is, different from us with different experiences, histories, talents, gifts, personalities and visions of truth and love. We need a constant self-transcendence through which, while not hiding the truth we see, we allow the truths others see to enter into our minds and hearts. If the Spirit continually instills this type of forgiveness in our hearts we will contribute to one another and all of us together will grow.

Cardinal Newman used to quote the saying of Saint Ambrose: *Non in dialectica complacuit Deo salvum facere populum suum.* ("God did not decide to save the world through arguments.") We all think our own positions and viewpoints are very logical. But Jesus is the very image of a man who quietly spoke and acted the truth that he saw. The vindication and sharing of that truth and vision came when he accepted death for his vision. On the cross he earnestly prayed for those who understood neither him nor his "threatening" vision of the Father's love: "Father forgive them for they know not what they do." Just as he was vindicated and transformed in his resurrection, so, in praying for our enemies, will we be transformed. "You can never really hate someone you pray for," said Dietrich Bonhoeffer. Through heartfelt prayer for those with whom we disagree, the Spirit of Truth and Love will dawn in our hearts.

The Church is the community of those who have committed themselves to Jesus' Lordship in human community. This implies a commitment to the purification of working through our conflicts with one another. Only with such a Spirit-given commitment will we have the patience to wait for the truth of another person to emerge. The Church is the community of those who live through, work through and suffer through such conflicts in order that the Truth that is Jesus can dawn on us

82

personally and as a community. Conflicts between laity and clergy, bishops and priests, theologians and all the others can be the occasion for a widening of our vision and our hearts.

When they are, it is Truth himself, the Spirit of Jesus, who is dawning upon us to give us a "sense," a "feeling," for the weight we give to one another's viewpoints. There should not be divisions in the Church of Christ, but tension itself is not unworthy of us. There are checks and balances among the different elements in the Body of Christ, as we all grow in age, in wisdom and in grace.

This more modest and patient view of conflict involves a confidence that the Truth is dawning on me, on my friends and on the community of those who want, who seek, who are open to all dimensions of reality. It implies a confidence in the truth that frees me from defensiveness and possessiveness in its regard. It doesn't mean I tolerate every opinion and every position as equally true and tenable. As was Jesus, we are called to speak the truth courageously and publicly before others, to label some opinions as false and others as true. But, with Jesus, we can do that with quiet confidence, "with authority," without defensiveness or an anger or lack of forgiveness that betrays our own insecurity.

SPEAKING ANOTHER'S SIN

Whenever we speak another's sin
we should do so with the very attitude of God,
his kindness and tenderness,
his forebearance,
his healing forgiveness.

The world speaks another's sin in
condemnatory fashion,
harsh and judgmental,
killing and not freeing.

We need your attitude so much, Lord,
in ourselves
and in one another.

FORGIVENESS

Then Peter went up to him and said, "Lord, how often must I forgive my brother if he wrongs me?" Jesus answered, "Not seven, I tell you, but seventy-seven times."   [Matthew 18:21–22]

Forgiveness is central to Christianity. In it the walls that separate us are broken down and the mercy of the Lord flows among us. Only to the extent that we sense and feel the mercy of the Good Shepherd in our own midst will we incarnate that mercy and forgiveness in our relations with each other. If our hearts have not experienced in the community of the Church the incredibly good news of God's special care for sinners it is unlikely that we will be bursting to tell that news to others.

What is needed, then, is a healing. If our hearts are bitter and resentful—whether or not we admit it to ourselves—if the problem is always "other people" or our approach to life is basically one of "blaming," then the basic condition of our hearts is hurt, wounded and untrusting. We are not free enough to forgive.

An example can be taken from a physical wound. If someone cuts us with a knife, our first need is to be healed of that wound. We need all our energy just to get well. Unless we can, we will not be free to think of the other person, free to begin to understand him and to forgive him.

In a somewhat similar way, the wounds of our hearts often extend far into our histories. What we need is, first of all, to recognize the wound. We cannot suppress it or pretend it does not exist. If we try to suppress this awareness, the wound will lead an underground life and our hearts will not be whole.

Many problems with authority in community are rooted in unhealthy family relationships. If our parents have neglected us or our hearts are starved for love, it is a real feeling and it is essential to acknowledge that. Only if we feel the wound (which may be due to our own excessive sensitivity), will the healing grace of Christ come into our lives. As one writer suggested, "No one really forgives another unless he bears the penalty of the other's sins against him."

Sometimes the pain of relationships is rooted solely in the diversity of personalities that God has created. There are "all the colors of the rainbow," all types and kinds of persons. Sometimes we are called to forgive someone just for being who he is—different from us.

The chalice raised at the Eucharist reflects the faces of the community around the table of the altar. It is in and through the blood of Jesus poured out for us that both our hidden and our manifest sins are forgiven and we are given the strength to forgive one another.

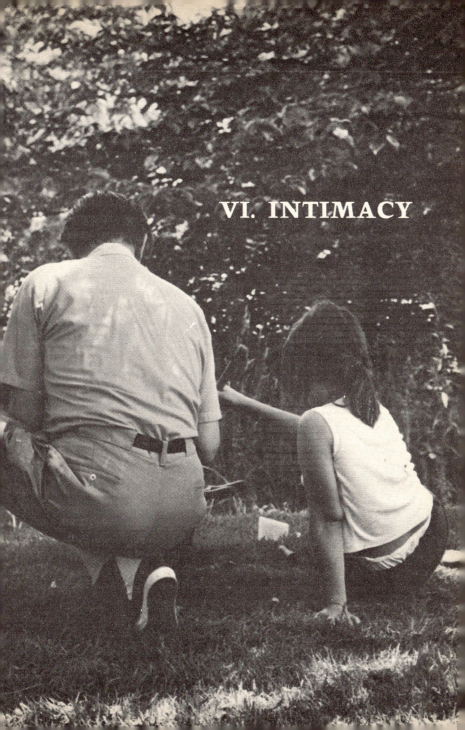

VI. INTIMACY

Menschenfreundlichkeit

But when the kindness and generosity of God our Savior dawned upon the world, then, not for any good deeds of our own, but because he was merciful, he saved us through the water of rebirth and the renewing power of the Holy Spirit. [Titus 3:4–5]

Jesus,
How much I need your tenderness, your gentleness . . .
"When the *Menschenfreundlichkeit* of God appeared . . . "
You were—you were (as the German says it)
the very friendliness of God with the human family. . . .
You are the Father's tender friendship with us.
Jesus,
In my heart . . .
in my life . . .
this day . . .
Thank you . . .
Through the Cross.

Jesus,
Sinner that I am,
Help me not to be afraid . . .
Help me
To be your *Menschenfreudlichkeit* to others.

FRIENDSHIP

The mystery of friendship is at the heart of Christian faith.

> A man can have no greater love
> than to lay down his life for his friends.
> You are my friends,
> if you do what I command you.
> I shall not call you servants any more,
> because a servant does not know
> his master's business;
> I call you friends,
> because I have made known to you
> everything I learned from my Father.
>
> [John 15:13–5]

Jesus' intimacy with his Father flows into his friendship with us. He wants to share with us everything that goes on between him and his Father. The communion of knowledge and love between them is offered to us.

It is in friendship that the deepest secrets of our hearts are unlocked. Only in self-abandonment to the other do we truly find ourselves, truly become ourselves. It is only through being loved and accepted for the mystery in me that is yet to be revealed that I will find out who I am. It does not happen overnight. It is the challenge of a lifetime.

That is why human friendship and human love are so very important. They reveal God's relationship to us. How else could we speak of Jesus' love for us if we had no glimmer of, no taste for, the gift of friendship in our own lives.

For that is what friendship is: a gift, a grace of unmerited, unearned but wonderful love.

LETTING BE

When you touch that which is closest to you,
That which gently and finely con-grooves with your
        own very spirit,
Your own very self
 . . . Then, be careful . . .
Do not rush at it forcibly, blinded by desire . . .
And thus miss it.
Do not smother it, grasping it and hugging it
violently to yourself . . .
Let it be
(him . . . her)
And let yourself be:
    paining
    open
    gentle with yourself
    and with the other
    proper distance to be
    and let the other be.
And if you're gentle with your own aching self
And allow the other to be,
Then the Lord of life will throw bridges of Spirit
        across the chasm
    which you yourself cannot cross
    without ruin.
Then the Lord of life, Cross-bridge (Pontifex),
    will throw the anchor of his love
    on thin fine threads
    that are stronger than death.
Praise him!

HUGGING

Grabbing . . .
  or
Lightly touching,
    freeing,
Heart to heart
    violence seeping
    through human arms,
Tenderness accepting
    shared pain.
Transformation.
    New Life.

GOD'S HEART-ACHE

The Suffering of each of our hearts—
Can we take it away from one another
    by our love for one another?
Or, in our love for one another,
    can we deepen
    the pain and suffering,
    so that
    it blends
    into the heart-ache of God
    for his world?

MARY

Oh Woman,
Draw me heavenward.
Reach gently,
Touch gently
the inner springs
of my life.
Gently, gently
Mother me
to be,
to stand.
Mother me to life,
Father, mother,
My life, wholeness
Sense, sensuous,
Holy, wholly human
Jesus.

VII. PRAYER

SOLITUDE

Solitude
　—pain.
Stillness bringing to light all of life
　　—memories, fears,
　　tragedies of heart,
　　faces,
　　broken trusts,
　　limits
　　—intimations of dead-ends—Evil.

Solitude—covered with His love:
　　"Trust me"—greater than your sins.
My passion for you is greater than your passion for
　　things.

　　Love caressed name,
　　feminine care,
　　heart love
　　for you—
　　Do you believe?
"Greater than this you will see."
　　No greater love,
　　Jesus.

Your worries, your fears
your unfigured-out situation.
　　Stop figuring!
　　I love you, and I will show you the Way
my Way,
　　the Way of my love.

　　Climb the tree of solitude to see me and to welcome me
into your house with joy!

RELIGIOUS PRACTICES

John Henry Newman once remarked on the feeling of joy many people experienced after long and tedious religious ceremonies. It was almost as if the length and tedium of the ceremony provided them with the opportunity of loving God more deeply. The ceremony was an opportunity to "practice" loving God, not just in spite of difficulty, but in and through difficulty.

Religious practices are specific ways in which the human person can truly "leave house and home and wife and children" in order to seek the Lord. Such leaving involves moving beyond one's worries as well as one's joys—whatever can capture and obsess us—in order to fall into the arms of the "Beyond." The Lord is the One who is beyond all our joys and sorrows and yet is present to us in our joys and our sorrows. Peter asked the Lord what was in it for himself and his friends. They had left everything to follow him. Jesus promised a hundredfold of everything they had left.

Ultimately, our need for religious practices is rooted in our need for God. If we love someone, we'll spend time with him. It is as simple as that: "Tell me where you spend your free time, and I'll tell you what you care for—or whom you care for." Time in prayer and recollection is time spent in developing this care for the God who deeply cares for us. The justification for prayer is the Lord.

Sometimes, however, we need to be shocked into prayer and the habit of prayer. Someone once said to me: "You better start praying or your life will end in a shambles." From that day I began the often painful process of sitting still with the Lord each day, calling out to him and wrestling with him, beginning to believe ever more deeply that the formation of that habit was his work in me.

Such habits of prayer and recollection are not just "law,"

although they can turn into that. It is not a question of "putting in time" because I have to complete an obligation: fifteen minutes or a half-hour a day that will enable me to "feel good" because I've done my duty. No, real prayer is a question of the heart. It comes from where I am. It is a living relationship with the living Lord. It is constantly changing and developing. Sometimes it reflects our needs and petitions; often it is filled with thanksgiving, responding to the hand of the Lord, the fruits of his Spirit in yesterday's or today's activity. Sometimes it involves entrusting the future to him.

In all of this an environment of prayer can be helpful. We are bodily beings, affected more than we realize, consciously and unconsciously, by the environment around us, by the places and sounds, the light and the darkness, the people we meet, the schedules we keep. Some lifestyles are so filled with distractions and confusion that there is little time or encouragement for the heart to be at peace or the mind to open up to the ways of God's love. An environment of prayer requires a time and space to pray, as well as the encouragement of other people to engage in this ongoing love-life with the living and loving God.

This is the importance of liturgy. The deepest level of our beings is influenced by the flow and direction of others' lives and liturgy symbolizes that flow and direction in our common bodily lives. By the setting of liturgy, the light and the darkness, the words and the prayers, the songs and the gestures, we are carried into a common love of God.

We need time for religious practices. Our bodies must begin to feel that the Father is very interested in us as his sons and daughters. We need time for prayer so that our hearts increasingly can believe that he loves us so much that he would have us, with Jesus, be channels of redemption for the world he loves. We need time for prayer so that our very beings can begin to believe that he is even more interested in solving the problems of our lives than we are.

99

REMEMBERING

Help me to remember you, Lord.

Remember you love me
    in the beautiful morning
    sun-bathed, fresh and open,
    mind-bathed
    and heart-soaked with your love
    perfumed with your eternal love.

To remember you love me at mid-day,
    perfuming again my heart
    with a sense, feeling, belief
    in your eternal, playful, free love
    no matter how seriously
    I take
    the sufferings, hurts
    and boredom
    of life.

And in the evening,
    five minutes
    to remember
    you love me.

And at night,
    to look to you
    and allow you to look at me
    sometimes lonely
    and in need
    of human love.

THE EXPERIENCE OF PRAYER

If the love of God, his "first love" for us, is the central reality of our lives, the context within which "we live and breathe and have our being," then recognizing and reverencing and thanking him for his love is central to being truly human. If his mercy and renewing power are important, then spending time, even "prime time," in prayer is a top priority. If we are to "shout from the rooftops what you hear in secret," then we must pray.

The Father's love never forces us. He only "attracts" us, "invites" us, knocks at the door of our hearts. The mystery of God's love is the "mystery of tenderness." It is quiet and gentle, yet in the long run very strong, strong enough to send a Francis Xavier to Asia, a Frances Cabrini to New York, New Jersey and Chicago, a Vincent de Paul and a Mother Theresa to the poor of their cities, a Dorothy Day to the poor of hers.

What, then, is prayer? In the last analysis, as a friend once remarked to me, it is "allowing God to love us." We don't have to—he doesn't force us—but we can allow him to be present to us in a free and conscious way so that he can care for us in his Spirit. "Raising our minds and hearts to God," we find that he has already lowered himself to us.

Prayer is allowing the mystery of tenderness symbolized in the Cross of Jesus to wash over our whole being, sink into the marrow of our bones in ways "too deep for words" and enlighten all the dark corners of our lives. The Spirit coming from the pierced side of Jesus can give us courage to face and accept all the hurts we have sustained from others and from the universe. Even more, it can give us the courage to face those we have afflicted on others.

Only the love of God deeply accepted in prayer—that is, in a heart totally open to God—can give us the courage to face

101

ourselves as sinners in human community, people who are insensitive to the sensitivities of others, misunderstanding, misjudging and even mistreating. Only God's mercy ever present in Jesus can illumine in prayer the broken promises to friends and acquaintances and give us the power to pick up the pieces and go on, hopefully with new power and new love.

"Lord, teach us to pray." All of us at times join the first disciples in that request, for all of us, at least at times, find it difficult to pray. What a relief, then, to read Saint Paul: "We really do not know how to pray, but the Spirit himself intercedes for us with sighs too deep for words" (Romans 8:26).

The first attitude we should have toward prayer, then, is to believe in it—no matter how poor ours seems to us. God loves us and has moved us to love. That happens in our hearts, beneath our words, where the Spirit becomes one with our spirit to join us to our Father. No matter how impoverished and puny our efforts at prayer, as long as we are groping, reaching out toward the Lord, the great act of his love for us is actually taking place in our hearts.

The prophets and psalmists of the Old Testament are great models of prayer, of a living relationship to the living God. Their prayer was not always beautiful. Often it consisted of very real sorrow, regret and even complaint: "How do evildoers prosper and the just man is afflicted?" It is sometimes good for us, like the psalmist, to tell the Lord how "unreal" he seems, how far away and distant his love feels.

Inevitably, if our relationship to the Lord is real, if we are talking to him in words and feelings, slowly but surely (although also at times quickly), we will be carried beyond our words by the Spirit "too deep for words." Such is the living silence of love. In our very desire for him he is already touching us. With Paul, we "stretch out to grasp hold of him who has already grasped hold of us" (Phil. 3:12). As our desire for him is inflamed, so too is the spark of his love ignited.

This is the most important aspect of our prayer, what writers have called its affective part. It is good if this totally "loving" part can be the beginning and the end of our prayer. Some of the saints spent long periods of time in silent wordless love. Sometimes their one word was "Jesus."

In addition to this affective aspect of prayer, there is also meditation. In it we drop "back to earth" from our affective union with the Lord. With that taste of love in our hearts, we allow the various aspects of the Gospel message and the various aspects of our lives to pass through our minds. The Gospels can reveal to us the deepest meaning of what is really going on in our families, our jobs, our towns. Similarly, these real situations from our lives can give flesh and blood (sometimes literally) to the Gospel message. At times an incident from our lives (a hurt, a hope, a joy) will be the subject of our prayer and certain phrases of the Gospel will help us to put it in the context of the Lord's love. ("Come to me, all you who labor ... " "I am with you all days ... " "Happy are the poor in spirit ... "). At other times, in more systematic fashion, we will begin from the Gospels and look for their meaning in the nitty-gritty of our lives.

The important thing about prayer is that we do it—even if for a while it is difficult. The honeymoon comes later with the Lord! Since he is who he is, it is not too much to give him our time. Just to be with the Lord bodily—to sit in a chair before him at the end of a day—is already an act of love for him. A mysterious process is underway whose fruits he promised would be a hundred-fold in this life and, in the world to come, life eternal. Would that we could give him a special time each day, a longer time each week and each month; and, finally, a genuine retreat each year. At such times we can allow his love into the core of our lives.

A friend of mine who has "learned to pray" told me that now others can tell when he has *not* prayed: He is easily depressed and, in general, unloving. Genuine prayer is not an escape from life but a meeting with the Lord of life which allows him to "conspire" with us in the loving decisions he is inviting us to make.

YOU ARE!

Headache

Busy
>   Many experiences, thoughts, meetings,
>   plans—
>   all crowding in on one another.

Need this time to separate the pieces
>   to find my heart
>   to find Jesus' heart
>   who has found my heart . . .

Jesus, revealer of the Father
>   in life
>   and love,
>   but especially in love,
>   so as to enliven life.

All these people . . .
>   functional relations . . . duties . . .
>   and love . . .

My friends . . .

And you, Lord—
>   *You Are!*

SILENCE

Most of us crowd too many people into our lives. There are too many events, even significant ones, too many cares, too many "important" things and people.

How much we need silence! Not empty agitated silence, not the silence of escape, but the silence in which we meet what is real, the silence in which we really meet the persons and events we have encountered.

"All real life is meeting," according to Martin Buber. But if all I do is meet people and events, my encounters become more and more fleeting and scattered. I fail genuinely to meet the persons I have met.

I am a body-person. My body, my feelings, my psyche, enter into every meeting I have. I need time, I need silence, to digest the events of my life. Silence that is filled with peaceful dynamism, silence that is filled with the mantra, with verbal psychic soothing, in which "music heard so deeply" begins to affect even my bodily being.

It is inescapable that the Father loves his children. Good Father that he is, he cares infinitely about every dimension of our being. He sent his only beloved Son to share our bodily being. Good Father that he is, he wants us to be touched and nourished by the bread-becoming-flesh of the Eucharist. He feeds us with himself!

Only deep silence, silence filled with God's own life, is capable of accepting this fact. Only deep silence can open our spirits to the Spirit. Then the Word can take flesh and dwell among us. Out of that silence those I meet are met as dimensions of the Word of God, guiding and forming history to bring us to the Father.

INTO YOUR HANDS

Jesus,
> Into your hands I commend my spirit.
> This day
> Whatever you want of me
> I want of me
> Waiting on you
> Falling into you
> Trusting you
> In the midst of my life.

Jesus,
> Into your hands I commend my spirit.
> This day
> This whole day
> Morning
> Noon
> Evening
> &
> Night.

Jesus,
> Into your hands
> Into your heart
> I commend my
> heart
> broken
> feeble
> distracted
> insecure & uncertain.

Jesus
> Into you
> I commend my
> self.

THANKS

Not rashly now

    but deeply.

Maturely?

    perhaps

    but still with a fear

    of being too brash.

Thank you, Lord

    . . . for everything.

VIII. JUSTICE

THE DEMANDS OF JUSTICE

> What is good has been explained to you, man; this is what
> Yahweh asks of you: only this, to act justly, to love tenderly and
> to walk humbly with your God. [Micah 6:8]

As Christians, we believe that to "act justly" we must be loved
into it. Justice flows from a humble God tenderly loving us into
loving beyond the close circle of our family and friends, out
into the wider circle of the human family. This "one love" that
we share with our God flows into all our relationships.

The prophets spoke of orphans and widows. Today we
speak of "the third world" and even "the fourth world," countries and the dispossessed of our own land. But it is the same
love that calls out to us from all the poor. It is Jesus who speaks
to us in the person of our poor neighbors. It is Jesus who speaks
to us from the ends of the earth.

I was hungry . . .

I was thirsty . . .

I was in prison . . .

There is only *one love*. It regulates and orders all others. It
teaches us to "love tenderly" our family and friends. It demands that we relate justly to all. There is among us the lure of
an absolute moral order that requires a deepening and widening consciousness of the demands of loving God's beloved people. Obviously, this means being sensitive and "nice" to the
people we live with and see daily. But it also means attending to
the life-styles and the social structures and institutions that ei-
ther help or hinder human growth and development through-
out the world. Christian conversion involves a growing awareness of the plight of God's people and a growing willingness and

111

commitment to put oneself out so that they may truly live. The Second Synod of Bishops in Rome, in 1971, made a startling assertion:

> Action on behalf of justice and participation in the transformation of the world fully appears to us as a constitutive dimension of the preaching of the Gospel.

This means being concrete. There are all kinds and levels of poverty even within our own experience—if we but have eyes to see. There are the senior citizens, workers laboring under severe economic pressures, young people seduced by the illusive lure of the media. There are the ostracized and the alienated.

In all of this there is the question: What does it mean to live a truly human life? Is it true in our day, as the title of the book suggests, that "small is beautiful"? Does a truly human life involve the central values of space for leisure and free time? Is some freedom from economic necessity essential for development of human talents, for truly human relationships, for truly human community? Is the new creation promised by Jesus in some kind of continuity with the divinely created structures of this creation? And what are those structures of truly *human* life?

The first effect of the coming of the Holy Spirit on Pentecost was the formation of the first Christian community with its sharing of life and even of material goods. Does being a Christian today involve some implications in our way of possessing material goods, our sharing them with one another, our defense of the poor and the alienated? The life style of Jesus himself and the central message he brought of divine presence in human poverty demands an affirmative answer.

This growing consciousness within Christian faith and belief is a far cry from mere moralism. True morality never imposes demands on people that they cannot meet. A moralistic approach to life overwhelms people with a "tyranny of shoulds," communication of guilt with no power of transformation. Gospel morality, however, begins from a sense of God's mercy toward us in Jesus Christ. He loves me . . . he knows me . . . he's forgiven me. He has given me life to enjoy—to "look at the birds of the air and the lilies of the fields"—and he has given me life to share. It is from such an awareness of God's yearning love that Gospel morality flows.

> If he has done all he could for me, can't I respond in kind?
> Can't I love this person?
> Can't I love these people by trying to make more lovable the conditions of their lives?
> Can't I work to make more livable the structures in which they live out their lives?
> And, perhaps, can't I tell them about the love that has loved me?